KU-657-182

Rough Guides
25 Ultimate experiences

USA

Make the most of your time on Earth

ROUGH GUIDES

25 YEARS 1982–2007
NEW YORK • LONDON • DELHI

Contents

Introduction

EXPERIENCES have always been at the heart of the Rough Guide concept. A group of us began writing the books **25 years ago** (hence this celebratory mini series) and wanted to share the kind of travels we had been doing ourselves. It seems bizarre to recall that in the early 1980s, travel was very much a minority pursuit. Sure, there was a lot of tourism around, and that was reflected in the guidebooks in print, which traipsed around the established sights with scarcely a backward look at the local population and their life. We wanted to change all that: to put a country or a city's popular culture centre stage, to highlight the clubs where you could hear local music, drink with people you hadn't come on holiday with, watch the local football, join in with the festivals. And of course we wanted to push travel a bit further, inspire readers with the confidence and knowledge to break away from established routes, to find pleasure and excitement in remote islands, or desert routes, or mountain treks, or in street culture.

Twenty-five years on, that thinking seems pretty obvious: we all want to experience something real about a destination, and to seek out travel's **ultimate experiences**. Which is exactly where these **25 books** come in. They are not in any sense a new series of guidebooks. We're happy with the series that we already have in print. Instead, the **25s** are a collection of ideas, enthusiasms and inspirations: a selection of the very best things to see or do – and not just before you die, but now. Each selection is gold dust. That's the brief to our writers: there is no room here for the average, no space fillers. Pick any one of our selections and you will enrich your travelling life.

But first of all, take the time to browse. Grab a half dozen of these books and let the ideas percolate … and then begin making your plans.

Mark Ellingham
Founder & Series Editor, Rough Guides

Ultimate
experiences
USA

South Beach occupies the southernmost part of Miami Beach. **Ocean Drive** runs south-to-north next to the sea for ten blocks. The best area for sunbathing is between 5th and 15th streets; any of the terraces along Ocean Drive are ideal for people-watching.

Scoping out the Scene on Ocean Drive

1 At sundown, the main promenading street of Miami's hedonistic South Beach was like a gigantic movie set, where different films were being shot simultaneously.

in a Gold's Gym tank-top weaved between the pedestrian traffic that crept past Ocean Drive's **swanky cocktail lounges**, thrusting his hips from left to right, a gasping Pomeranian struggling to keep up. Cheesy gay porn sprang to mind. Crossing the road to the beach side of Ocean Drive brought the area's famed **Art Deco buildings** perfectly into view – a strip of pastel yellows, blues and oranges bathed so dramatically in the fading sunlight that you could have been standing in the middle of a Disney cartoon.

As sunbathers gradually started to leave the beach, a couple of **real-life Barbie dolls** with tiny waists and enormous chests lingered on the sand to be filmed for some dubious Internet site. The poolside at the Clevelander was filling up with **Spring Break schmoozers** and girls with plenty of potential for **going wild**. The electronic music that earlier had drifted gently from hotel lobbies was now being pumped out in energetic beats, heralding the **transformation** of twilight's **languorous Ocean Drive** into nighttime's **frenetic strip of revelry**. Clubbers flashed synthetically **manufactured smiles** as they hurried to the latest **place to be seen**; pretty hostesses talked to you when you stopped to have a look at the expensive restaurant menu they were touting; and the waitress at the Kent scribbled her number on a napkin when the **three Latinos from the Mustang** slapped down a generous tip.

Just another day in the neighbourhood.

A 1978 Mustang pulled up outside the **Kent Hotel** and three Latino men, designer shirts unbuttoned **almost down to the navel** and sporting heavy gold chains, stepped out in what could have been a scene from *Scarface*. A bronzed, male rollerblader

Catching a
2 baseball game

Home to an iconic outfield wall rung with ivy, not advertisements, Chicago's Wrigley Field is where America's pastime reaches its apotheosis. Though it dates to 1914, it's not the oldest ballpark in the major leagues, nor is it the smallest (both honours go to Boston's equally famed Fenway Park, opened two years earlier). And as for team play – well, the kindest thing to say is that the stadium and the fans that fill it have borne witness to some hard times. The home-team Cubs haven't won a World Series since 1908, the longest such streak by four decades. But for baseball purists, there's no better place to properly enjoy a game.

Nicknamed "The Friendly Confines" by Cubs' legend Ernie Banks, the idiosyncratic park anchors the buzzing neighborhood of Wrigleyville. The stadium melds perfectly with its surroundings: along Waveland Avenue, fans wait just outside the low outfield wall hoping to catch a stray home-run (and throw it back on the field, if it's hit by the opposing team), and the views from adjacent apartment rooftops – some sporting grandstands – are better than from the faraway seats in mega-parks elsewhere.

Inside, the game feels more like a mammoth picnic than a high-stakes competition, particularly during summer afternoon contests. (The park didn't add lights until 1988, and the majority of Cubs' home games are still played under the sun.) It's no stretch to say that fans expect to have fun rather than win: after all, why should things change now? So get a cheap seat with the so-called "Bleacher Bums" and join in the raucous sing-along of "Take Me Out to the Ball Game" during the seventh-inning stretch. If the Cubs don't win, it's really not such a shame.

at Wrigley Field

need to know

Most games at Wrigley sell out. Scalped tickets can be had, but your best bet is to purchase tickets weeks in advance from the team itself (☎773/404-2827, ⊛www. cubs.com); prices range from $15 to $55 per seat. If you can't get a ticket, pull up a stool at *Murphy's Bleachers* or *Sheffield's*, two of Wrigleyville's finer watering holes.

Making like King Kong

THE EMPIRE STATE BUILDING has been lauded as the pinnacle of the Art Deco style in the 1930s, hit with an American bomber during World War II and used as a staging point by failed parachutists, aerial suiciders and, of course, an oversized Hollywood simian. However, you don't have to have a flair for drama to visit – just a taste for glorious views and a clear lack of acrophobia.

Provided you can endure the tedious queues at the base, when visiting you'll have two choices: take the conventional route to the 86th-floor observatory or pay a little more and add another sixteen storeys to your ascent. The latter 102nd-storey observatory sits just below the building's spire and near its T-shaped mooring units, built for the structure's short-lived use as a blimp dock. Yet while its height is certainly impressive

need to know:
The Empire State Building, 350 Fifth Ave (daily
8am–midnight; last elevators 11.15pm). Tickets
are $16 for the 86th-floor observatory (buy them
at the site or online; ⓦwww.esbnyc.com) and $14
more for the 102nd-story observatory (buy them
from the second-floor ticket office).

the observatory's glass-enclosed views and cramped confines don't
do justice to the stunning panorama of New York laid out before your
eyes.

For a 200-mile view of the terrain – both leafy green and steely
modern – save your money and choose the 86th floor option. Exposed
to the biting wind in the cooler months and always crowded with
onlookers, this story's observatory is nevertheless hard to beat for a
visual spectacle. Aside from trying to figure out what Connecticut looks
like in the distance or identifying Manhattan's many steel and mirror-
glass boxes, you can also take a big gulp and look straight down to
see the building's magisterial facade dropping a thousand feet below
you. You can't stray too far up here, but you can peer out just enough
to get an unobstructed view of the skyline of one of the world's great
cities.

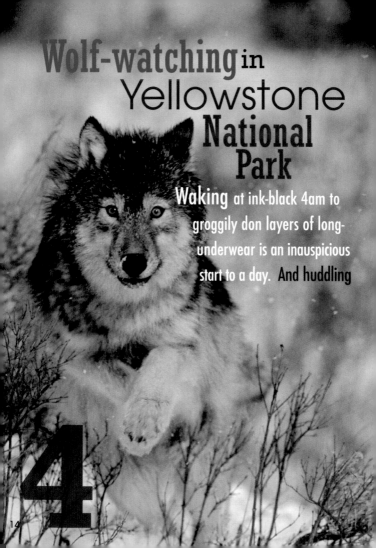

Wolf-watching in Yellowstone National Park

Waking at ink-black 4am to groggily don layers of long-underwear is an inauspicious start to a day. And huddling

4

14

with strangers on a roadside turnout a half-hour later, shivering against the well-below **FREEZING** temperature, hardly sounds better. But as a crack of light on the horizon grows and an eerie chorus of **HAIR-RAISING HOWLS** rises from the gloom ahead, your discomfort is soon forgotten. The morning's **WOLF-WATCH** is already a success. When it was founded in 1872, Yellowstone was celebrated as a **WONDERLAND OF GUSHING GEYSERS**, where elk and bison roamed freely. But while visitors flocked to the world's first national park to glory in the steady steam of Old Faithful, indigenous animals believed to be a danger to both man and more cuddly creatures were **TRAPPED AND KILLED** at virtually every opportunity. **GRAY WOLVES** were particularly feared, and the last pack was exterminated in 1926. For nearly seventy years, wolves, once the continent's most **ABUNDANT PREDATOR,** were absent from the country's most prized ecosystem. It took until the winter of 1995 for the first group of Canadian gray wolves to be trucked in under the Roosevelt Arch. The reintroduction program has been a **RUNAWAY SUCCESS** and, as of writing, about 150 wolves roam here. Thanks to the high density of prey, a single pack in Yellowstone can live within less than fifty square miles, making the park the world's most reliable place in the wild for watching wolves. The **LAMAR VALLEY**, where the wolves were all originally released, remains the **BEST SPOT** to catch a glimpse of these complex and social creatures, who rely on teamwork to **TAKE DOWN PREY IN BLOODY BATTLES** but also to raise new pups each spring. Even if you're not fortunate enough to see a wolf, you'll get to interact with the omnipresent wolf-watching parties clustered along the park's highways, exchanging stories of favorite wolves and **DRAMATIC HUNTS** between peeks through a line of spotting scopes.

need to know
Rates for wolf-watching tours (☏307/344-2294, ⊛www. yellowstoneassociation.org) average $80–100 per day, not including accommodation. Interpretive classes are held within the Lamar Valley's Buffalo Ranch.

5
Touring Graceland

As pilgrimages go, touring Graceland isn't the most obvious religious experience. The Memphis home of legendary rock-and-roll star Elvis Presley doesn't promise miraculous healing or other spiritual rewards. But for those who perceive truth in timeless popular music – as well as in touchingly bad taste – a visit to the home of "the king" is more illuminating than Lourdes.

From Elvis's first flush of success (he bought the house in 1957 with the profits from his first hit, *Heartbreak Hotel*) to his ignominious death twenty years later, Graceland witnessed the bloom and eventual bloat of one of America's biggest legends. Just as he mixed country, gospel and rhythm and blues to concoct the new sound of rock-and-roll, Presley had an "anything goes" attitude toward decorating. The tiki splendour of the jungle room, which has green shag carpeting on the floor and the ceiling, is only steps from the billiards room, where the couch and the walls are covered in matching quilt-print upholstery. In the living room, a fifteen-foot-long white sofa sets off a glistening black grand piano. (The audio tour commentary, from Lisa Marie Presley, is understandably preoccupied with her father's impetuous shopping habits.) Amid all the glitz, though, you can still glimpse an underlying humility. A modest, windowless kitchen was one

of the King's favourite rooms, and the blocky, colonial-style house itself is nothing compared to today's mega-mansions, especially considering he shared the place with his extended family for decades. The quiet, green grounds are a respite from the less-than-attractive patch of Memphis outside. And even after passing through a monumental trophy room and a display of Elvis's finest jewel-encrusted jumpsuits, you can't help but think that this was a man who hadn't strayed too far from his rural Mississippi roots.

Serious pilgrims pay their respects at Elvis's grave, set in the garden at the side of the house. Around the mid-August anniversary of the singer's death, tens of thousands flock here to deposit flowers, notes and gifts – an homage to a uniquely American sort of saint.

need to know
Graceland, 3734 Elvis Presley Blvd (March–Oct Mon–Sat 9am–5pm, Sun 10am–4pm; Nov daily 10am–4pm; Dec–Feb Mon & Wed–Sun 10am–4pm; ☎800/238-2000, ⓦwww.elvis.com/graceland). Tours range from $22 to $55.

"**GENTLEMEN, start your engines**!" With that, the crowd noise crescendos to a **deafening roar** and 33 cars line up to await the start of the most thrilling speedway race in the world. The numbers **boggle the mind**: five hundred tension-filled laps, speeds topping off around 230mph, more than half-a-million spectators, $10 million-plus in prize money. The Indy 500 is an **electrifying** experience, not to mention the event that best embodies the American obsession with getting **somewhere** FAST – in this case, right back where you started.

Visitors come for the **glitz and glamour** as well as the **star-power** of legends like Mario Andretti, hailed as the greatest driver of all time, who conquered Indy in 1969 and now watches his sons, grandson and nephew compete. But the race is not without its homespun **midwestern charm**: rather than a champagne spray, the winner's celebratory libation is…milk, a tradition since 1937, after three-time winner Louis Meyer **chugged** a glass of **buttermilk** in Victory Lane the year before. The garage area is still referred to as Gasoline Alley, even though the cars run on methanol, and the final practice race is known as "Carb day," despite the switch to fuel-injection systems.

If the **earsplitting** noise and **heart-stopping** speeds don't provide enough of a rush, pivoting your foot on the accelerator of a real 600 horsepower V-8 Nascar certainly will. The BePetty School of Racing allows you to experience firsthand the **thrill** of Indy-car racing on the actual Indy track. After being kitted out in racing suits, each class of around twenty aspiring Andrettis is given a **crash course** in safety, driving instructions and an introduction to the philosophy of "trust the car" before competing for the fastest average lap speed. If you're blood's not racing when you step out of the car, you must be **made of stone**.

6

need to know
The **Indianapolis 500** (⊛www.indy500.com) is held over Memorial Day weekend at the **Indianapolis Motor Speedway** (⊛www .brickyard.com), six miles from downtown. You'll need to pre-order tickets (starting around $80) for race day. The **BePetty School of Racing** (⊛www.1800bepetty .com) "Rookie Course" costs $525.

Hitting the Track at the Indianapolis 500

Hiking
Half Dome in
Yosemite

7

Five hours after

your dawn start from Yosemite Valley, you're still not at the top of Half Dome, whose looming, truncated form ("like it had been sliced with a knife") makes it one of the most iconic mountains in North America. The sun is beating down, you're dehydrated, and the most challenging section is still ahead. In front of you lies a vast curving sheet of virtually smooth gray granite rearing up at an impossibly steep angle. There's no way you'd get a grip in even the best sticky-rubber hiking boots but, fortunately, some determined souls have forged the way, drilling holes in the ancient rock and attaching a series of cables and wooden steps. Help yourself to a pair of leather gloves stashed at the base of the "staircase", grab the cables and haul your way up the final 400ft to the 320-acre summit plateau. It's an exhilarating finish to a superb hike.

From the top, nearly 9000ft up, the dramatic views will render you speechless. Those who dare can edge toward Half Dome's

need to know
From the trail to the top of **Half Dome** and back (17-mile roundtrip; 9–12hr; 4800ft ascent) will take most people all day. Get an early start to cover most of the serious ascent in the cool of the morning. Alternatively, book a place in the **Little Yosemite Valley campsite** about halfway up and make it a two-day trip.

lip and dangle their feet over the side, while the very brave (or very foolish) may inch out along a projecting finger of rock for a vertiginous look straight down the near-vertical facade. But neither is necessary to appreciate how far you've come. Just turn to gaze back at your route along a section of the famed 212-mile John Muir Trail; even the two magnificent waterfalls you passed – the Vernal and Nevada falls – look puny from this height. Then take in the snowy spine of the Sierra Nevada mountains, the rippling granite sheets that run up to the summit of Cloud's Rest and the wonderland of forests and alpine meadows that comprise Yosemite National Park.

Skiing at Snowbird and Alta

Alta and Snowbird, downhillers searching for skipped **BOTTOMLESS POWDER** know better than to follow suit. Squeezed side-by-side at the upper end of Little Cottonwood Canyon, the resorts first linked their lifts the same winter the Games kicked off in nearby Salt Lake City; ever since, their nearly 5000 combined acres have added up to the **FINEST downhill skiing** experience in North America. Like two brothers forced to share a bedroom, the resorts have learned to coexist while maintaining their distinctive characters. Alta, the little resort that

8

could – or, better yet, wouldn't – opened in 1939. Since then little has changed, and therein lies Alta's **charm**: while other resorts LOUDLY EMBRACE all thing modern, anachronistic Alta tenaciously holds onto its old-world lodges, **CREAKY** double-chair lifts and ban on snowboarding, prizing tradition over convenience at nearly ever turn. Opened forty years later, brash Snowbird next door welcomes boarders and any other **DAREDEVILS** willing to ride the thrilling aerial tram zipping nearly 3000 vertical feet up to the crest of Hidden Peak. **Steep-and-deep** is the quickest way to describe the riding here, where a ski-it-if-you-can ethos prevails.

Granted, you won't find a hip village like nearby Park City, or the glitzy crowds that flock to Aspen and Vail in Colorado at either resort. Instead you'll encounter **LAIDBACK DOWNHILLERS** happy to spend their time exploring a **spine-tingling** collection of chutes, cirques, cliffs, and **knee-knocking** steeps that can leave even the most hardcore enthusiast humbled. Softening the inevitable **spills**, an epic 500 inches of yearly snowfall forms **fluffy pillows** of light, desert-air snow. So much snow can dump at once, in fact, that breakfast is often accompanied by the deep, pleasing boom of World War II-era howitzers blasting away at fresh snow, readying the slopes for a morning filled with first-tracks through **DEEP POWDER.**

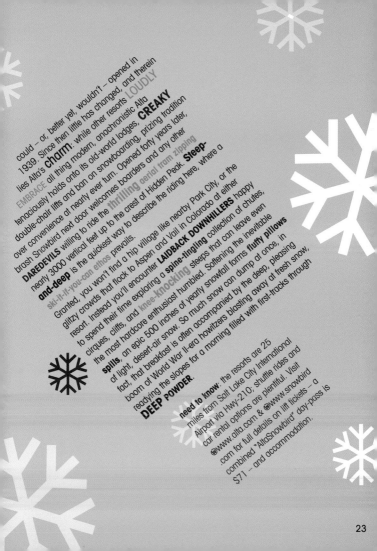

need to know: the resorts are 25 miles from Salt Lake City International Airport via Hwy-210; shuttle rides and car rental options are plentiful. Visit @www.alta.com & @www.snowbird .com for full details on lift tickets – a combined "AltaSnowbird" day-pass is $71 – and accommodation.

...UNTIL JUSTICE ROLLS DOWN LIKE WATERS
AND RIGHTEOUSNESS LIKE A MIGHTY STREAM

MARTIN LUTHER KING JR

Tracing civil rights history in Montgomery, Alabama

THE STRUGGLE FOR AFRICAN-AMERICAN CIVIL RIGHTS – one of the great social causes of American history – played out all across the South in the 1950s and 60s. To try to gain a grasp on its **legacy**, and a sense of how the fabric of the country has still in a way **never quite healed**, make your way to Montgomery, Alabama, the culmination of the so-called Selma-to-Montgomery National History Trail.

Start at the state capitol building (which looks like a cross between the US Capitol and a plantation manor), and where you can almost hear Dr Martin Luther King Jr in 1963 declaring at the end of the four-day Selma-to-Montgomery civil rights march, "however difficult the moment, however frustrating the hour, it will not be long, because truth pressed to earth will rise again". To experience more of **King's spirit**, take in a **passionate Sunday service** at the Dexter Avenue King Memorial Baptist Church, where today's ministers use King's example to inspire both parishioners and casual visitors. The church's basement holds a mural depicting scenes from King's life, as well as his preserved desk, office and pulpit. His birthplace, for those interested, is in the Sweet Auburn district of Atlanta, Georgia.

The Rosa Parks Museum honours the Montgomery event that started it all. Parks's refusal in 1955 to accept a seat at the back of a Montgomery bus in essence **sparked the civil rights movement**; her inspiring story is told through photographs and dioramas, and you can step onto a replica of that city bus. Most poignant, though, is the **civil rights memorial**, centred on a black-granite table designed by Maya Lin and inscribed with the names of forty activists killed by racist violence from 1954 to 1968. The events described on the table are as good an overview of the era as you're likely to find.

9

need to know
Alabama state capitol, 600 Dexter Ave (Mon–Fri 8am–5pm); **Dexter Avenue Church**, 454 Dexter Avenue (℡334/263-3970, ⊛www .dexterkingmemorial.org). **Civil Rights Memorial**, 400 Washington Ave (open 24 hrs; free); **Rosa Parks Museum**, 252 Montgomery St (Mon–Fri 9am–5pm, Sat 9am–3pm; $5.50). **Civil Rights Memorial Center** (Mon–Fri 9am–4:30pm, Sat 10am–4pm; $2; ⊛www.tolerance.org /memorial).

10 Witnessing power in action in Washington DC

need to know
The White House (ⓦwww .whitehouse. gov /history/tours) can only be toured in a group of ten or more, with reservations made months in advance. Get tickets for free tours of the **US Capitol** at a kiosk on the building's southwest side (Mon–Sat; ⓦwww .aoc.gov/cc/ visit). **Supreme Court** sessions (Oct–June, 10am) typically last 1hr per case.

Dominated by massive monuments, museums, war memorials and statues, Washington DC represents the purest expression of political might. But the seat of government of the world's only superpower is a surprisingly accessible place – it's by the people, for the people, after all – and though certain security measures may seem an obstacle, you shouldn't miss the chance to see the corridors of power, and maybe even catch a glimpse of the action.

Wherever you go in DC, it'll be hard to avoid the looming, cast-iron dome of the **US Capitol** building. From its marvellous Rotunda (styled after Rome's Pantheon) to the stately figures of National Statuary Hall, you won't be disappointed (and may be slightly awed) by the country's centre of legislative power. For an upclose look at the angry speech-making and partisan posturing of Congress, however, you'll need to get a special pass in advance of your trip.

Although "Dubya" and his advisors stay well out of the public eye, you can still tour the seat of the executive branch, aka the **White House**. The Georgian Revival home of the president is full of historical furnishings and rooms decked out in various styles; if you reserve far enough in advance, you can check out sights like the richly draped, chandeliered East Room, the silk-trimmed and portrait-heavy Green Room, the oval, French-decorated Blue Room and a glittery display of the presidential china.

Perhaps the most rewarding spot for actually seeing American government at work is the US **Supreme Court**. The building itself is stately enough, with its grand Greek Revival columns and pediment, but the real sight is all nine justices arrayed behind their bench, meticulously probing the lawyers making their arguments. From these arguments the Court writes its opinions, affirming or striking down existing laws and at times making history before your very eyes.

With its rolling green hills, bucolic landscapes and small towns heavy on antique charm, California's Wine Country, centring on Napa and Sonoma valleys, is one of the most beautiful places in the West. Beyond touring the wineries – Beringer, Silver Oak, Stag's Leap, Robert Mondavi and many more, all of which allow you to sample the goods – there's no shortage of things to see and do. Come here for a weekend retreat (preferably not at the peak of summer, when the hordes descend), and your first instinct might be to pack in as much as possible. But in a place where the main point is to relax, indulge and melt away the stresses of modern life, that's the last thing you should do.

Instead, aim for just a few choice tastes of the good life. Start with a spot of nature, either driving the Silverado Trail (parallel to Hwy-29), taking in the mountains and vineyards along the way, or enjoying a peaceful walk through the woods in Jack London State Park, once ranchland owned by the famed naturalist writer. Next, rest your aching bones and revitalize your senses by checking into one of the resort spas near Calistoga. At **Dr Wilkinson's Hot Springs**, dip yourself in a mix of heated mineral water and volcanic ash, or at **Mount View Spa**, enjoy the mud baths and herbal applications, as well as aromatherapy, hydrotherapy and other refined New Age treatments that pamper both the body and soul.

Round out your experience with a great, even legendary, meal at one of the region's many gourmet restaurants; these days the place is known as much for food as the vino. Foremost among these is **Thomas Keller's French Laundry**, an icon of California Cuisine known for its blend of fresh local ingredients and creative, spellbinding presentation. It won't come cheap and you'll have to reserve months in advance, but it's reason enough to visit.

need to know

Dr Wilkinson's Hot Springs, 1507 Lincoln Ave, Calistoga (☎707/942-4102, ⊛www.drwilkinson.com); **Mount View Spa**, 1457 Lincoln Ave, Calistoga (☎707/942-5789, ⊛www.mountviewspa.com). **Jack London State Park**, Glen Ellen (⊛www.jacklondonpark.com; $6 per vehicle). **The French Laundry**, 6640 Washington St, Yountville (☎707/944-2380, ⊛www.frenchlaundry.com).

11
Spending a weekend in
California wine country

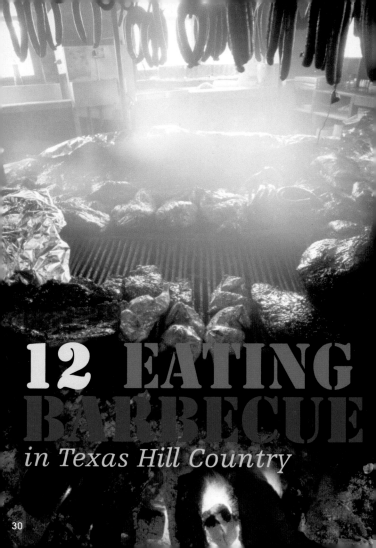

12 EATING BARBECUE

in Texas Hill Country

If you think barbecue is a sloppy pulled-pork sandwich or a platter of ribs drowned in sticky sweet sauce, a Texan will happily correct you. In the rolling hills around Austin – where pecan trees shade the road, pickup trucks rule and the radio is devoted to Waylon, Willie and Merle – barbecue reaches its quintessential form. It is nothing but pure, succulent meat, smoked for hours over a low wood fire, preferably in a brick oven seasoned for generations. In fact, at one veteran vendor in Lockhart, the management maintains a strict no-sauce policy, so as not to distract from the perfectly tender slabs of brisket. Your meat, ordered by weight, comes on butcher paper with nothing to dress it up but crackers.

Thankfully, this austerity applies only to the substance – not the quantity – of the meat. Gut-busting excess is what makes barbecue truly American, after all, especially at places like the legendary Salt Lick southwest of Austin near the town of Driftwood. The all-you-can-eat spread includes heaps of the standard beef brisket, pork ribs, and sausage, all bearing the signature smoke-stained pink outer layer that signifies authentic barbecue. On the side, you get the traditional fixin's: German-style coleslaw and potato salad, soupy pinto beans, sour pickles, plain old white bread, and thick slices of onion.

So whether you visit the Salt Lick, the Kreuz Market (those anti-sauce hardliners in Lockhart), Black's (another Lockhart gem, which has conceded to a light sauce), Louie Mueller's (in an old wood-floor gymnasium in Taylor), City Market (in Luling), or any of the other esteemed purveyors a local barbecue fetishist points you to, don't ever forget: it's all about the meat.

need to know: In Lockhart: **Kreuz Market**, 619 N Colorado St (Mon–Sat 10.30am–8pm; ☎512/398-2361); **Black's Barbecue**, 215 N Main St (Mon–Thurs & Sun 10am–8pm, Fri & Sat 10am–8.30pm; ☎512/398-2712). In Luling: **City Market**, 633 E Davis St (☎830/875-9019). Near Driftwood: **The Salt Lick**, 18001 FM 1826 (daily 11am–10pm; ☎512/858-4959, ⓦwww.saltlickbbq.com). In Taylor: **Louie Mueller BBQ**, 206 W 2nd St (Mon–Sat 10am–6pm; ☎512/352-6206. Most places are cash

13

Sitting at the northern edge of America's Rocky Mountains, magnificent Glacier National Park's craggy cliffs, awe-inspiring peaks and beautiful deep-blue lakes are, true to the park's name a result of massive tongues of ice invading the land from the north some 20,000 years ago. While the trails through this magical terrain are stunning – leading you past colourful mountain meadows, towering columns of rock up to 1.6 billion years old and all manner of elk, bighorn sheep, mountain goats and grizzly and black bears – you can also gaze at some of the park's best, and most harrowing, views along the Going-to-the-Sun Road.

Cutting across the middle of the park, connecting the wooded groves of Montana's Rockies with the sprawling dry expanse of the Great Plains, the road offers an eye-popping jaunt over the Continental Divide itself, where at Logan Pass (6680ft) there's a visitors' centre and a chance to stretch your legs in the shadow of the park's mighty peaks. By the time you get there, you'll have ascended from the low-lying charm of Lake MacDonald to gently rolling foothills, to a sudden series of switchbacks that rise ever higher with each mile.

The stunning views from the road as it contours along the jagged face of the Rockies feature sheer precipices that drop far down into shadowy forests, frozen rivers of ice framed by stark canyon walls and splashing waterfalls fed by snowmelt. While the road can be perilous at times, its narrow width straining to accommodate passing cars and its sheer-edged drop-offs not allowing much room for driving error, a white-knuckle ride is simply not possible, due to the slow speed of traffic during the peak summer season and most drivers being so overcome by the visual splendour that they forget about things like speed, direction or destination.

need to know
The most popular entrance to **Glacier National Park** (ⓦwww.nps.gov/glac) is near the town of West Glacier, off Hwy-2. Park admission is $25 per vehicle (half that for those on foot or bike), but is good for seven days; another $5 buys a year-round pass.

Going to the sun
in Glacier National Park

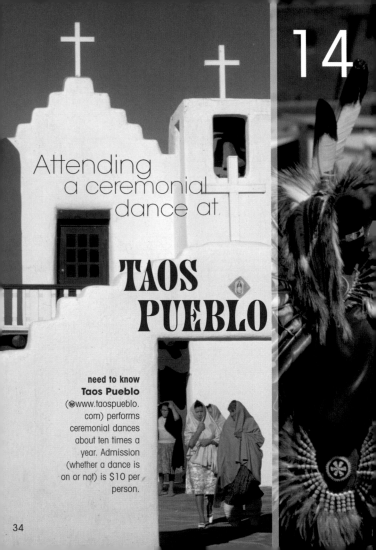

14

Attending
a ceremonial
dance at

TAOS
PUEBLO

need to know
Taos Pueblo
(ⓦwww.taospueblo.
com) performs
ceremonial dances
about ten times a
year. Admission
(whether a dance is
on or not) is $10 per
person.

The sun shines down from the cloudless turquoise sky, but your feet are cold. You stamp them impatiently, squint your eyes against the glare and tuck your mitten-swaddled hands under your armpits. The rest of the crowd seems unconcerned, even though the scheduled starting time was surely hours ago, so you continue breathing in the freezing air, fragrant with wood smoke, and watching your breath cloud in front of you. Inside the adobe church Christmas Mass has come and gone, and people mill around the open plaza greeting friends and chatting quietly, the elders and women settling into folding chairs with blankets over their laps or wrapped around their shoulders. Or they begin to pay holiday visits inside the mud buildings that rise up, in haphazard stacks, three or four stories high. Beyond the soft edges of the ancient pueblo stands the hard blue Taos Mountain.

And then, from the direction of the mountain, you hear a distant drone. The murmuring crowd goes quiet. The muffled drumbeats grow clearer, the rhythmic shimmer of bells joins in, and you forget about your feet. The waiting throng forms a border around the pueblo's sacred dance space, instinctively giving prime spots to residents of this thousand-year-old settlement. The crowd parts easily when the procession of men arrives – they are no longer men but deer, their antlers swinging, their dainty hooves picking at the earth. As the drums boom and the chanting swells, the transformation is complete – the circle is a forest glade, and hunters trace the edges, taking aim with their symbolic arrows.

Hours pass, or perhaps only minutes, and then the drums stop. The illusion lifts: these are mere men, some boys, laboring under slippery elk hides, many of which look as though they were butchered only this morning. Shirtless, the men are breathing hard from the rigor of the hunt, giddy and sombre at the same time. The women now take their place in the circle, making delicate hand motions with switches of piñon tree, and you stamp your feet again, tuck your hands tighter, and surrender once more to the heart-pounding drums.

WATCHING the fish fly

It's not every day that you see a twenty-pound King salmon being heaved through the air. The curious pastime is done by large men in butcher smocks who bellow with each throw, occasionally missing their targets (the open arms of other large men in butcher smocks) and ending up with their finned projectile bouncing across the concrete or, even better, into the lap of a gaping tourist. And while it may be an uncommon sight to most, it's just another day in Seattle, in the bustling agora of the Pike Place Market.

But the crazy, sometimes violent, seafood spectacle here is far from the market's only emblematic sight. There's the charming plump figure of the brass pig, an oversized piggy bank at the market's entrance that draws money for charity; the very first Starbucks, dating from 1971, with its original racy, bare-chested mermaid logo intact; and the grand neon letters of the market sign itself, whose soft red glow has popped

up in a handful of movies, *Sleepless in Seattle* being the most famous.

As the signature market in the Pacific Northwest, Pike Place is anything but a simple array of agricultural stands: it's a virtual rabbit warren of stairways, corridors and

at Pike Place Market

to old-timers to down-and-dirty punk rockers. Its array of eclectic vendors includes the Sub Pop Megamart for indie rock, Left Bank Books for radical reads, Three Girls Bakery for delectable pastries and more java joints, ethnic diners and

cantilevered storeys built into the hillside of the Seattle waterfront, a teeming mass of clubs, bars, restaurants and shops. The market has been here for a century, but only since it was almost demolished in the 1970s has it gone on to become the signature attraction of the Emerald City to visitors and locals alike – everyone from upscale yuppies

cherry, berry and apple dealers than you can imagine. And if all else fails, there's always the fishmongers, who can get you anything from salmon and trout to marlin and halibut – just be sure to duck.

Fresh

need to know
Pike Place Market, 1st Avenue and Pike Street (Mon–Sat 10am–6pm, Sun 11am–5pm; many clubs and restaurants have later hours; @www.pikeplacemarket.org). Fish-throwing is from around 11am to noon or later.

16

Strolling through downtown
Savannah, Georgia

need to know
Walking tours ($10–20) cover everything
from local architecture to legends noted
in John Berendt's book *Midnight in the
Garden of Good and Evil*. Visit ⓦwww
.savannahvisit.com for a full list of options.

When an intrepid British utopian named James Oglethorpe founded Savannah in 1733, he thought he could tame the local marshes and alligators without the aid of slaves or – more preposterous – hard liquor. The latter ban fell by the wayside less than twenty years later, and Savannahians have been devoted to immoderation ever since. Any walking tour of the three-square-mile downtown historic district should, for tradition's sake, be accompanied by a cold beer in a perfectly legal "to-go cup". (The traditional local tipple, Chatham Artillery Punch, is more safely appreciated sitting down, however.)

One element of Oglethorpe's vision that did stick was the city's layout – a repetition of grids and squares that have become 21 miniature parks, each offering a different proportion of dappled shade, fountains and monuments. In the springtime, when azalea, dogwood and honey-rich magnolia trees are in full bloom, the squares are at their most alluring. But even in the thick of an August heat wave, when the air is like a sauna and the greenery is growing wildly up the cast-iron balconies, the squares offer a respite from the untamed mugginess. The sunlight shimmers through the craggy oak boughs and Spanish moss, the cicadas drone and cars motor laconically around the cobblestone streets. The stately homes that face each square represent all of the most decadent styles of the eighteenth and nineteenth centuries: Neoclassical, Federal, Regency, Georgian, French Second Empire, and Italianate.

"The Belle of Georgia", as the city is known, hasn't always been so; for much of the twentieth century, decadence had slipped into outright decay. But in 1955, seven elderly ladies banded together against developers to defend the 1821 Davenport House from being turned into a parking lot, and the Historic Savannah Foundation was born. Fortunately, no such effort is required of today's casual visitor – you just need to stroll and sip your drink and watch the centuries roll by.

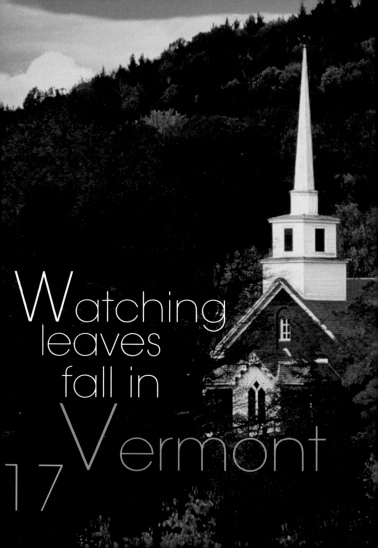

Watching
leaves
fall in
Vermont
17

Vermont's Route 100 winds its way

through quintessential New England scenery, skirting tidy chocolate-box villages nestled beneath the Green Mountains, dotted with white-steepled churches, clapboard houses and homemade sweets shops where the owner knows you by name. But from late September to early October, when the leaves start to change colour, the road is transformed into a two-hundred-mile, skin-prickling display of arboreal pyrotechnics; it's as if the entire state has been set ablaze. Even the most die-hard cosmopolitan will find it hard not to be seduced by the spectacular scenery, as dizzying peaks give way to a conflagration of vermillion sugar maples, buttery aspens, scarlet sourwoods and acid-yellow ashes.

This yearly riot of colour can be appreciated whether you choose to ever leave your car or not. Gliding along a winding stretch of open road, crawling through an impossibly picturesque nineteenth-century town, or off-roading along serpentine country lanes, the explosion of unreal-looking leaves is inescapable – and unadulterated (no billboards or malls are allowed along the route). For an up-close look, pull off Route 100 and head into Green Mountain National Forest to walk along part of the 265-mile Long Trail, which has countless leaf-peeping opportunities alongside rugged, mountainous terrain, flowing streams and placid ponds.

need to know

The first two weeks of October are prime leaf-viewing time, but you can usually see the colours change later in the month – it depends on the weather and what part of the state you're in (®www.foliage-vermont.com should keep you updated). Whichever town on Route 100 you choose to stay in, make sure to book far in advance – note you'll have better luck during the week than on weekends.

BREAKING the
bank in
Las Vegas

18

No matter how you arrive in Las Vegas, whether by plane or lonely desert drive, you'll never forget your first sight of Sin City. The neon jungle appears out of nowhere, and once you get into the belly of the beast – look, the Eiffel Tower! the Statute of Liberty! – if anything it's even more impressive. The true miracle of Vegas, however, is the way in which it can chew you up, spit you out and send you packing convinced that you've had the time of your life.

As you walk along the Strip, bursts of cool air and the sound of money spewing from machines tempt you to enter a casino. When a showgirl in a feather boa appears and hands you a free buffet voucher, you decide to take the plunge. Once inside, a sense of well-being envelops you. The air-conditioning feels so good after trudging along in 100° heat and the cocktail waitresses seem to be giving out free drinks. Flashing signs proclaim this particular casino to have "The loosest slots in Vegas", and this happy coincidence makes you fumble in your pocket for change. A few quarters later and you get your first big win. Your malevolent alter ego takes over. He orders you a drink and directs you to the roulette wheel. You start to make modest gains. Cheers from the craps table, a shimmering Lamborghini on a revolving pedestal and the croupier's swift fingers distract your attention while Lady Luck leaves by the back door. You put your last chip on black. It's red.

It must be getting late, but you can't find a clock anywhere; it's dark outside when the casino finally lets you go. You're down a week's wages, but all you can think about is returning tomorrow to win the Lamborghini and spend that forgotten buffet voucher – and about how you had the best time of your life.

need to know

Las Vegas's casinos are open 24hr but you must be over 21 to play. Minimum bets at the table games are usually $5 or $10. The casino has the mathematical advantage in every game.

19

Reconsidering the *Wild West* in

When you think of the American West, it's hard to conjure a more iconic image than Monument Valley, with its awesome mesas, spires of jagged sandstone and arid, desert-like plains. This is the Wild West of popular culture – a vast, empty landscape dating back to antiquity that can make you feel at once tiny and insignificant and completely free and uninhibited. These qualities have made it the perfect location for Westerns, which is perhaps why it seems so familiar: *Stagecoach*, *The Searchers*, *How the West Was Won*, and *Once Upon a Time In the West* are among the numerous movies that have been filmed here.

But while Hollywood favours heroic cowboys on stallions, you won't be restaging the gunfight at the OK Corral while here (head south to Tombstone, Arizona for that). Instead, this is sacred Indian country

Monument Valley

managed by the Navajo Nation, and to visit the area today is to experience the West through their eyes. From the Anasazi petroglyphs in Mystery Valley to the traditional hogans still inhabited by local Navajo, every rock here tells a story. The valley's most famous formations – like the twin buttes of the Mittens, with their skinny "thumbs" of sandstone, and the giant bulk of Hunt's Mesa – can be seen from the circular, seventeen-mile track (starting at the visitors' center) that's usually smothered in red dust. Navajo guides, who fill you in on local history and culture, lead 4WD rides around the track, as well as longer, usually overnight, expeditions by foot. These may start before dawn, allowing you to reach the top of a mesa before it gets too hot and watch the sunrise across a land where sand and rock stretch endlessly before you to the horizon.

Angered by the completion of Mount Rushmore in 1941, a group of Lakota Sioux chiefs led by Henry Standing Bear asked sculptor Korczak Ziolkowski to build a monument to the Native American legend known as Crazy Horse: victor of The Battle of the Little Big Horn; a leader who never signed a treaty; and a warrior who never surrendered. Mount Rushmore, just seventeen miles down the road, was big – this had to be bigger. As Henry Standing Bear put it, "we want to let the white man know we have heroes too".

The first thing that hits you when you gaze upon the memorial, deep in the Black Hills of South Dakota, is indeed its enormity. While the images of Mount Rushmore were carved onto existing rockface, Ziolkowski reshaped an entire mountain, blasting, drilling and carving, slab by slab, an image of the revered warrior atop his horse, his arm stretched over the land he fought to defend in the 1870s. The modern Orientation Center is over a mile from the 563ft peak, so initially you won't even grasp the memorial's true dimensions, but take a bus to its base and you'll be utterly mesmerized.

It's not just the proportions that are overwhelming. The audacious, seemingly hopeless timescale of the project makes the great Gothic cathedrals of Europe seem like prefabs. When Ziolkowski died in 1982, his family continued the work he had begun 34 years earlier; Crazy Horse's face, with its finely shaped nose and eyes, measures 87ft tall and was completed as recently as 1998. Today, his horse is gradually taking shape through a series of blasted-out ridges, but it's impossible to estimate when everything will be finished. No matter though: time seems to have little significance here, as the construction work – careful, reverential – has become almost as sacred as the monument itself.

20

need to know: the **Crazy Horse Memorial** is open daily 8am–4.30pm in winter and 7am till dusk in summer, when there's a laser and multimedia show. Entrance is $10 for adults (free for kids under 6) or $25 per car.

Checking the progress of the Crazy Horse Memorial

Slicing through some of the most stunning scenery in the country, the Blue Ridge Parkway winds its way along the crest of the Appalachian Mountains, from the Shenandoah National Park in Virginia to the Great Smoky Mountains National Park between North Carolina and Tennessee. Once dotted with isolated frontier communities where bluegrass was born, today you'll find traces of the region's history – like old gristmills, abandoned wooden barns and ramshackle diners – scattered along the road, but in truth much of what has been preserved is aimed squarely at the tourist trade. What the parkway is best for is simply a heavy dose of nature at its finest.

The first part of the drive cuts through northern Virginia, and here the ridge is very apparent, sometimes reducing to a narrow ledge not much wider than the road. The central section is much less dramatic – the land is heavily farmed and the road busier with local traffic, especially around Roanoke. But the lower highway, which snakes through North Carolina, is the most spectacular part. There's plenty of kitsch development here (the town of Blowing Rock is a full-scale resort, with shopping malls and themed motels), but the views are astonishing – at nearby Grandfather Mountain, on Hwy-221 one mile south of the parkway, a mile-high swinging bridge hangs over an 80ft chasm with 360° views.

Further south, near Mount Pisgah, the road reaches its highest point. As you ascend toward it you'll have numerous chances to stop at overlooks, or just pull onto the shoulder, for breathtaking vistas: hazy blue ridges, smothered in vast swathes of hickory, dogwood and birch and groves of mountain ash bursting with orange berries.

Riding high *on the* Blue Ridge Parkway

need to know
The parkway starts at
Rockfish Gap near
Waynesboro, Virginia, just
off I-64, and ends 469 miles
later near **Cherokee**, North
Carolina, on Hwy-441. The
speed limit is 45 miles
per hour. Fall is the most
popular time for a drive, to
see the changing leaves.

A FAR CRY from glamorous Aspen and Vail, yet close to both, the basic cabins of the 10th Mountain Division Hut System – named in honour of the US Army ski corps that trained here during World War II – offer a unique look at Colorado's backcountry, and an atmospheric alternative to a typical alpine vacation. A stay in any one of them (there are 29 in total) grants you access to the pristine sawatch mountains and a slice of some 350 miles of underused cross-country skiing, snowshoeing, hiking and mountain-biking trails within central Colorado's prime national forest.

Although you won't be using the soldiers' hickory-board skis and striking out with ninety pounds of gear on your back, the hut system is still about simplicity and making your way in the wild. Accommodation is basic, equipped with mattresses, wood-burning stoves and rudimentary cooking facilities. Your water will come from melting snow, and you'll be bunking down with sixteen or so strangers that typically share a hut. A normal day might be spent very unassumingly – taking a few runs on nearby slopes, heading back to your hut to warm up by the fire, then venturing out again to build a snowman or go sledding before settling in to cook a simple dinner, and perhaps making some new friends while you're at it.

While it's the self-sufficient, back-to-nature aspect of this experience that makes it so memorable, the other side is that you're at nature's mercy. You'll need to be prepared: in the event of an emergency, it can take a good six hours before help arrives. You may tire quickly at the high altitudes and become confused by whiteouts in the fading light of dark winter forests as you search for elusive way-markers. You'll need to be fit, have great gear and adequate wilderness skills. But once you pass muster at nature's boot camp, that stylish ski resort may never hold the same appeal.

Hit the hut:
22 attending nature's boot camp in Colorado

need to know
Huts can be booked through the **10th Mountain Division Hut Association** (☎970/925-5775; ⓦwww.huts.org; $25–40 per person per night). Alternatively, **Paragon Guides** (☎970/926-5299 or 1-877/926-529, ⓦwww.paragonguides.com) run fully supported mountain biking and Nordic skiing trips between the huts (from $990 for three days).

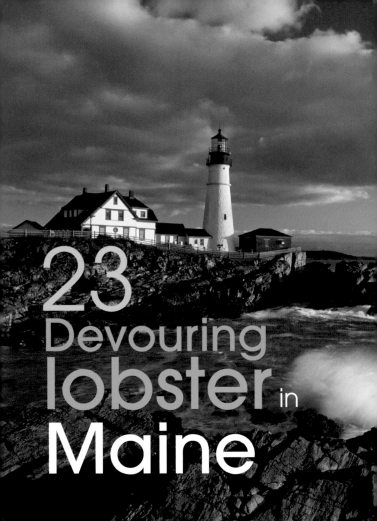

23
Devouring
lobster in
Maine

You're seated at what must be one of the most picturesque spots in the country: a rustic picnic table outside of an unassuming, clapboard restaurant, with a storybook lighthouse to your left and craggy cliffs pummeled by an unruly sea to your right. Maine's slogan is "The Way Life Should Be", and here, situated along its gorgeous, corrugated coastline, you can't help but agree. That is, of course, if you're able to think of anything other than the red, hot challenge in front of you – one freshly steamed Maine lobster, waiting to be cracked open and savoured.

Eating Maine lobster is a culinary rite of passage for visitors to the state. It requires tools (nutcracker, teeny-tiny fork), patience and enough hubris to believe that you can look cool even while wearing a disposable bib. It's smart to bring along an experienced lobster slayer; your first lobster can be intimidating, and it's nice to have a bit of guidance (as well as someone to take that requisite embarrassing photograph).

Now you're ready to begin. Crack the claws in half, pull out the meat with your little fork, and dip it in the butter sauce. Lobster meat comes well-defended, so be wary of hot, sharp points along the shell. The tail follows the claws: tear it from the body, pushing the meat from the end. Finally (now that you're feeling emboldened), pull off the legs to suck out the last bit of flesh. There is no other meat like lobster – tender, sweet, elusive – and in Maine, where lobster is king, the crimson crustacean is celebrated with parades, festivals and an energetic devotion that's shared by everyone.

At its best, a lobster dinner should be an all-around sensory experience. Breathe in the salty ocean breezes. Listen for the booms coming from the lighthouse. Finally, lick the butter off your fingers, remove the bib and give your dining partner a high five – you've just taken part in a Maine institution.

need to know
There are numerous spots for great lobster across the state. Try **Two Lights Lobster Shack**, 225 Two Lights Rd, Cape Elizabeth (five miles south of Portland).

America's most over-the-top and hedonistic spectacle, Mardi Gras reflects as much a medieval, European carnival as it does a drunken Spring Break ritual. Behind the scenes, the official celebration revolves around exclusive, invitation-only balls; for such an astonishingly big event, it can seem put on more for locals than the revellers who descend on the town, but you'll hardly be wanting for entertainment or feeling left out.

Following routes of up to seven miles long, more than sixty parades wind their way through the city's historic French Quarter. Multi-tiered floats snake along the cobblestone streets, flanked by masked horsemen, stilt-walking curiosities and, of course, second liners – dancers and passersby who informally join the procession. There's equal fun in participating as there is in looking on.

Whichever way you choose to see it, you'll probably vie at some point to catch one of the famous "throws" (strings of beads, knickers, fluffy toys – whatever is hurled by the towering float-riders into the crowd); the competition can be fierce. Float-riders, milking it for all it's worth, taunt and jeer the crowd endlessly, while along storied Bourbon Street, women bare their breasts and men drop their trousers in return for some baubles and beads.

As accompaniment, the whole celebration is set to one of the greatest soundtracks in the world: strains of funk, R&B, New Orleans Dixie and more stream out of every bar and blare off rooftops – no surprise, of course, considering the city's status as the birthplace of jazz.

You might have thought that all of this madness would have been curtailed in the wake of Hurricane Katrina, but like the city, the party carries on in the face of long odds; indeed, the year following, many of the weird and wonderful costumes were made from the bright blue tarps that have swathed so much of New Orleans since the storm.

need to know: Mardi Gras (Fat Tuesday) is the night before Ash Wednesday, but the term is used loosely to refer to the whole of **Carnival**, which runs for six weeks beginning on Twelfth Night. For more information, visit Ⓦwww. mardigras.neworleans.com.

Getting in line

at MARDI GRAS

As you manoeuvre your way toward the towering face of one of Alaska's many tidewater glaciers, the gentle crunch of ice against the fibreglass hull of your kayak sounds faintly ominous. It's nothing, though, compared to the thunderclap when a great wall of cracking ice peels away from the face and sends waves surging toward you. Your first reaction is quite naturally a jolt of fear, but no need to panic: if you're at least 500 yards away from the glacier face (as any sensible paddler is), the danger will have dissipated by the time whatever's left of the waves reaches you.

Watching glaciers calve while paddling round a frozen margarita of opaque blue water and brash ice is an undoubted highlight of sea kayaking in Prince William Sound. Perhaps better still are the opportunities for viewing marine life here. Seals often loll around on icebergs close to glaciers, while sea otters swim in the frigid waters protected by the wonderfully thick fur that made them prized by the eighteenth-century Russian traders who partly colonized Alaska. In deeper water, look for pods of orca, which cruise the waterways searching for their favourite food, seals (no wonder they hang back on the icebergs). You might even spot a few humpback whales, which congregate in small groups and breach spectacularly on occasion. Keep a splash-proof camera handy at all times.

Even if you miss out on a great action photo, there is considerable pleasure in just gliding around the generally calm waters of the fjords, where cliffs clad in Sitka spruce and Douglas fir rise steeply from the depths. For full atmospheric effect, stay in one of the simple Forest Service cabins or camp out on a small beach or at a designated campsite in one of the state marine parks; it's a wonderfully relaxing way to while away a few days – falling sheets of ice aside, of course.

need to know: Alaska Sea Kayakers (☎907/472-2534, ⓦwww.alaskaseakayakers.com) rent sea kayaks in plastic (single $40 a day; double $55) and fibreglass (double $60). They also run guided day-trips ($120) and multiday tours (around $300 a day).

25 Sea kayaking
in Prince William Sound

Ultimate experiences
USA
miscellany

1 People

The US has a population of **300 million**, of whom 67% are non-Hispanic white, 13% black, 5% Asian and – by far the nation's fastest-growing group – 14% Hispanic (or Latino), counted as an ethnic, not a racial, category.

The **biggest cities** are, in order, New York City, Los Angeles, Chicago, Houston and Phoenix – with the latter also the country's fastest-growing major city. The **fastest-shrinking** major cities are Detroit, Boston, Cincinnati, St Louis and New Orleans.

2 States and regions

The United States comprises four major regions:

Region:	% of US pop:	# of states:	Largest state:
South	36	13	Texas
West	23	13	California
Midwest	22	13	Michigan
Northeast	18	11	New York

The country's extreme geographical points are:

	Overall:	In the lower 48:
North	Point Barrow, AK	Northwest Angle, MN
South	Ka Lae, HI	Ballast Key, FL
East	West Quoddy Head, ME	West Quoddy Head, ME
West	Attu Island, AK	Cape Alava, WA

3 Music

Popular musical styles that have developed in the US include ragtime, blues, jazz, R&B, soul, doo-wop, hip-hop, zydeco and gospel (all derived from African-American culture) and bluegrass, country, Cajun and Appalachian folk (all derived from white Southern culture). The most famous hybrid of the two strands is **rock and roll**.

▶▶ According to *Rolling Stone* magazine, the **greatest rock albums** made by Americans are:

Pet Sounds, Beach Boys

Highway 61 Revisited, Bob Dylan

What's Going On, Marvin Gaye

Blonde on Blonde, Bob Dylan

The Sun Sessions, Elvis Presley

"In America nothing dies easier than tradition."

Russell Baker

 Hotels

▶▶ Five great hotels

Hotel Bel-Air, Los Angeles, CA. Set in a lush, isolated canyon in the elite confines of Bel Air. The most luxurious hotel on the West Coast.

The Carlyle, New York, NY. A grand Upper East Side landmark with a fine view of Central Park, genteel service and classically styled rooms and suites.

The Hay-Adams, Washington DC. Elegant Renaissance Revival icon overlooking the White House since the 1920s.

The Phoenician, Scottsdale, AZ. Among the country's best resorts, in the shadow of Camelback Mountain.

The Peabody, Memphis, TN. Luxury downtown hotel listed on the National Register of Historic Places. Famous for its resident ducks, who parade to and from the lobby twice a day.

5 Hotter than hot

The lowest, hottest and driest points in the US are in California's **Death Valley**. Badwater basin is 282 feet below sea level, while the ironically named Greenland Ranch reached 135°F in 2001 (the highest temperature ever recorded in the US and the second-highest in the world). Death Valley's overall average precipitation is less than two inches per year.

6 Thanksgiving

Thanksgiving has been officially observed in the US since the Civil War, though its legend dates back to 1621 as part of a goodwill ceremony between English Pilgrims and Wampanoag Indians in Plymouth, Massachusetts. Although the original meal may have involved venison, clams, dried berries and eels, modern Thanksgiving **dinners** traditionally include the following:

- One large turkey
- Bread or mushroom stuffing
- Mashed potatoes with gravy
- Sweet potatoes/yams
- Cranberry sauce
- Creamed onions

- Green beans or Brussels sprouts
- Waldorf or other salad (Waldorf salad is typically apples, celery, walnuts and mayonnaise)
- Rolls or biscuits
- Pumpkin/pecan/apple pie(s)

"I wish the bald eagle had not been chosen as the representative of our country… The turkey is a much more respectable bird, and withal a true original native of America."

Benjamin Franklin

7 Skyscrapers

▶▶ The five tallest US buildings are:

Building:	Location:	Height:	Built in:
Sears Tower	Chicago	1451ft	1974
Empire State Building	New York City	1250ft	1931
Aon Center	Chicago	1136ft	1973
John Hancock Building	Chicago	1127ft	1969
Chrysler Building	New York City	1046ft	1930

Chicago was also the home of the world's first skyscraper, the 1885 Home Insurance Building (now demolished). The tallest building on the West Coast is the US Bank Tower in Los Angeles, at 1018 feet.

8 Presidents

There have been 42 US presidents; however, since one, Grover Cleveland, was elected twice (non-consecutively), George W. Bush is considered the 43rd president. Presidents serve four years in a term and have a two-term limit.

Gerald Ford is the only person in US history to have served as vice president and president **without having been elected** to either position (he was appointed to both positions after the resignations of Spiro Agnew and Richard Nixon, respectively).

Because US presidents are elected by electoral votes and not popular votes, four men have become president **without receiving the most votes** from the people: John Quincy Adams (1824), Rutherford B. Hayes (1876), Benjamin Harrison (1888) and George W. Bush (2000).

"In America, anyone can become president. That's one of the risks you take."

Adlai Stevenson

9 Rivers

Of America's quarter-million rivers, the longest are the:

Missouri (2540 miles)
Mississippi (2340 miles)
Yukon (1980 miles)
Rio Grande (1900 miles)
St Lawrence (1900 miles)

"The tree of liberty must be refreshed from time to time with the blood of patriots and tyrants."

Thomas Jefferson

10 The Movies

According to the American Film Institute, the **greatest movies** ever made are:

Citizen Kane (1941). Orson Welles's groundbreaking tale of power, corruption and tragedy, based on the life of publishing magnate William Randolph Hearst.

Casablanca (1942). Hollywood's most romantic wartime saga, with unforgettable characters played by Humphrey Bogart and Ingrid Bergman.

The Godfather (1972). Francis Ford Coppola's blood-soaked epic that single-handedly revived the gangster genre and made stars of Al Pacino, Robert Duvall and James Caan.

Gone with the Wind (1939). This Civil War spectacular, with perhaps as many detractors as fans, is one of the most influential films of all time.

Lawrence of Arabia (1962). David Lean's sweeping tale of the Middle East adventurer who managed to strike a deep chord with Americans of the Kennedy era.

The **worst** American film ever made is generally acknowledged to be **Plan 9 from Outer Space** (1959), Ed Wood's classic sci-fi schlock-fest that, perversely, also has fans claiming it among the best – or at least most fun – films ever made.

The five highest grossing American films of all time (US box office, not worldwide), are **Titanic** (1997), **Star Wars** (1977), **Shrek 2** (2004), **ET: the Extra Terrestrial** (1982) and **Star Wars: Episode I – The Phantom Menace** (1999).

Great American filmmakers **never to have won an Oscar** for directing include Orson Welles, Stanley Kubrick, Martin Scorsese and Robert Altman.

11 Hand gestures

The only hand gesture that carries much weight in the US is the classic (and offensive) "bird", featuring an aggressively raised middle finger. While most international gestures may receive only a laugh, if anything at all, other prominent gestures include:

Gesture:	Meaning:
raised thumb and pinky/little finger	"Hang loose!"
raised index and middle fingers	"Peace" or "Victory"
raised index finger and pinky/little finger	devil horns (used mainly at heavy-metal concerts)
index finger pointing and twirling near temple of head	"Cuckoo" (she or he is crazy)
fist with protruding upward thumb	"Thumbs up" (good)
fist with protruding downward thumb	"Thumbs down" (bad)
fist held up in air	"Black power!"
index finger in open mouth	"Gag me" (for repellent things)
open hand with index finger and thumb making a circle	"OK" (ie, good)
rubbing thumb and index finger	money in general
crossed index and middle fingers	"Good luck", or to avoid a jinx
four fingers raised and split in half	"Live long and prosper" (for Trekkies)

12 Political parties

Two parties dominate politics in America. The **Democratic Party** is the world's second-oldest still-functional political party, dating from 1792 when it was known as the Democratic-Republican Party. Today's **Republican Party** formed in 1854.

Once prominent political parties that no longer exist include the Federalist, Anti-Federalist, Anti-Masonic, Whig, Know-Nothing, Free Soil, Populist and Progressive.

"A lie can travel halfway around the world while the truth is putting on its shoes."

Mark Twain

13 Cuisine

One of the more refined American cooking styles, **California Cuisine** was pioneered in the 1970s by Alice Waters of *Chez Panisse* in Berkeley and Michael McCarty of *Michael's* in Santa Monica. Borrowing from French *nouvelle cuisine*, the California variant emphasizes fresh, local ingredients, creative presentation and novel combinations. California Cuisine predates New American Cuisine, which brought these notions to a wider national audience starting in the 1980s. Other – and typically heartier – regional American cuisines include the following:

Indigenous cuisine:	Signature dish:	Culinary capital:
Barbecue	ribs/brisket	Texas
Cajun	jambalaya	New Orleans, LA
Creole	gumbo	New Orleans, LA
Hawaiian	poi (mashed taro root)	Honolulu, HI
Native American	fry bread	multiple
New England	clam chowder (cream based)	Boston, MA
Southern	grits (boiled milled corn)	Atlanta, GA/ Charleston, SC
Southwestern	chili con carne	Arizona/New Mexico
Tex-Mex	fajitas	South Texas

14 War

The United States has been involved in **eleven major wars**:

The Revolutionary War (1775–1783)
The War of 1812 (1812–1815)
Mexican-American War (1846–1848)
Civil War (1861–1865)
Spanish-American War (1898)
World War I (1917–1918)
World War II (1941–1945)
Korean War (1950–1953)
Vietnam War (1965–1973)
Persian Gulf War (1991)
Iraq (2003–present)

15 State mottos

California	Eureka!
Kansas	To the stars through difficulties
Maine	I direct
Maryland	Manly deeds, womanly words
Massachusetts	By the sword we seek peace, but peace only under liberty
Michigan	If you seek a pleasant peninsula, look around you
Montana	Gold and silver
New Hampshire	Live free or die
New Mexico	It grows as it goes
New York	Excelsior!
Oregon	She flies with her own wings
Texas	Friendship
Utah	Industry
Virginia	Thus always to tyrants
West Virginia	Mountaineers are always free

16 Ethnicity

The most common American ethnic backgrounds or ancestry are:

German (19%)

Scottish/Scots-Irish (15%)

Hispanic/Latino (14%)

Irish (11%)

English (8%)

Italian (6%)

Scandinavian (4%)

Polish (3%)

Americans of African, Asian and North American extraction come from a variety of ethnic groups, with any one group numbering less than 1% of the total population.

17 Religion

Approximately 77% of adults in America identify themselves as Christian (with Catholicism the largest denomination); 2% are Jewish; one-half of 1% are Muslim and approximately the same percentage Buddhist. Fourteen percent claim no religious affiliation.

▸▸ Five largest cathedrals

Cathedral of St John the Divine, New York, NY. Work began on this staggering Gothic Revival gem in 1892, and it's still under construction.

Washington National Cathedral, Washington DC. This beautiful neo-Gothic monument is perched on a hill above the nation's capital.

Basilica of National Shrine of the Immaculate Conception, Washington DC. America's biggest Catholic church, with vivid mosaics, cavernous spaces and a striking Romanesque style.

Cathedral of St Paul, St Paul, MN. Granite-and-marble jewel with a copper dome and elegant Old World effects in the unlikely setting of the upper Midwest.

Cathedral of All Saints, Albany, NY. Towering Episcopal church dating from 1888 and designed in the English Gothic style.

"The business of America is business."

Calvin Coolidge

18 Art

The first major art exhibit in the US was the Armory Show, or the "International Exhibition of Foreign Art," held in New York City in 1913. Reaction was not favorable – Teddy Roosevelt proclaimed, "That's not art!" But the US would catch up after World War II with the rise of **Abstract Expressionism**, the first American style to have a global reach. The movement, based in New York, was personified by figures such as Jackson Pollock, Willem de Kooning, Robert Motherwell, Mark Rothko and Clyfford Still.

Today, arguably the **greatest art museums** in the country are (in alphabetical order):

Museum:	Location:	Strengths:
Art Institute of Chicago	Chicago	American
Getty Center and Villa	Los Angeles	European and classical antique
Metropolitan Museum of Art	New York City	everything
Museum of Modern Art	New York City	modern American and European
National Gallery of Art	Washington DC	classic European, modern American

Across the American West, you can see huge pieces of a relatively modern technique known as **land art**, such as:

Name:	Artist:	Location:	Description:
City	Michael Heizer	SE Nevada	huge earthworks
The Lightning Field	Walter de Maria	West New Mexico	400 steel rods
Roden Crater	James Turrell	near Flagstaff, AZ	carved-out volcano
Spiral Jetty	Robert Smithson	Great Salt Lake, UT	spiraling rock jetty
Untitled	Donald Judd	Marfa, TX	art in abandoned sites

19 Television

According to *TV Guide*, the greatest American **television shows** in history are, in order, *Seinfeld*, *I Love Lucy*, *The Honeymooners*, *All In the Family*, and *The Sopranos*. The worst, in reverse order, are *Hogan's Heroes*, *The Brady Bunch Hour* (variety show), XFL football, *My Mother the Car* and *the Jerry Springer Show*. Recent figures claim the average American watches 4 hours and 32 minutes of TV per day – equivalent to 14 years of viewing for the average lifespan.

20 Sports

Most popular spectator sports:
Football (American)
Baseball
Basketball
Auto racing
Hockey

Most popular participant sports:
Swimming
Bowling
Fishing
Golf
Basketball

"Whoever wants to know America had better learn baseball."

Jacques Barzun

21 Climb every mountain

Aside from California's **Mount Whitney**, all of the twenty tallest mountains in the US are in **Alaska** – crowned by **Mt McKinley**, also known as Denali, at more than 20,000 feet. Colorado has 54 mountains more than 14,000 feet in height. The **shortest** of any state's highest "mountain" is **Britton Hill** in Florida, topping out at 345 feet.

22 A dog's life

Americans' favourite pets are **dogs** (36% of households have at least one), **cats** (32%), **birds** (5%), and **horses** (2%). Dogs are favoured by all income groups and households – except those living alone, who favour cats.

"America is great because she is good, and if America ever ceases to be good, America will cease to be great."

Alexis de Tocqueville

23 Literature

The idea of the "Great American Novel" – a work that perfectly reflects the character and culture of the nation – dates back to the Civil War era; every now and then some new book gets trumpeted as such, especially anything written by Phillip Roth or John Updike. Eight of the more enduring candidates include:

Invisible Man, Ralph Ellison. The greatest, and most depressing, portrait of race relations in mid-twentieth-century America.

The Sound and the Fury, William Faulkner. The quintessential Southern writer's masterwork, told from four different perspectives in four wildly different styles.

The Great Gatsby, F. Scott Fitzgerald. Perhaps the most formally influential American novel, rich with the rhythms and colours of the Jazz Age.

Moby-Dick, Herman Melville. A regular contender for *greatest* American novel, tells a gripping tale of survival, salvation and society on the high seas.

The Catcher in the Rye, J.D. Salinger. Perenially controversial tale of an angry, dejected youth whose travails have found an echo in the minds of young readers everywhere.

The Grapes of Wrath, John Steinbeck. Dust Bowl-era California is brought to life through the struggles of the Joad family as they navigate the bleak sharecropping world of the Great Depression.

The Adventures of Huckleberry Finn, Mark Twain. Still complex and challenging after 120 years, the signature tale of life on the Mississippi River in antebellum America.

Slaughterhouse Five, Kurt Vonnegut. The most experimental of the country's greatest novels, blending a brutal wartime saga with time travel and a fractured narrative.

"Have faith! Go forward!"

Thomas Edison

24 Crosstown traffic

Four of the five busiest urban freeways are in **Los Angeles** – the 405, 5, 10 and 101– along with Atlanta's I-75. The 405 carries nearly 400,000 cars a day.

The average American drives more than 8300 miles per year and annually emits two to five tons of **carbon dioxide** per vehicle.

According to *Bicycling* magazine, Portland, Oregon, is America's top city for bicycling, followed by San Diego, Denver, Seattle, Madison (Wisconsin) and Boulder (Colorado). The worst are Atlanta, Houston and Boston.

25 Festivals

Of the thousands of festivals that annually take place across the country, the following showcase some of the more unusual regional pursuits and pastimes:

World Grits Festival, St George, SC (mid-April). Consuming corn porridge in the grits-eating capital of the world.

Toad Suck Daze, Conway, AR (early May). Amphibian racing.

Solstice Parade, Seattle, WA (mid-June). Nude bike-riding.

Redneck Games, East Dublin, GA (early July). Hillbilly Olympics, featuring seed spitting and bobbing for pig's feet.

Lumberjack World Championships, Hayward, WI (late July). Climbing, sawing and rolling logs.

Testicle Festival, Missoula, MT (mid-Sept). Devouring bulls' balls.

Punkin' Chuckin', Millsboro, DE (early Nov). Hurling pumpkins by catapult.

Doo-Dah Parade, Pasadena, CA (Sun before Thanksgiving). Goofy anti-Rose Festival.

Ultimate
experiences
USA
small print

ROUGH GUIDES – don't just travel

We hope you've been inspired by the experiences in this book. To us, they sum up what makes the USA such an extraordinary and stimulating place to travel. There are 24 other books in the 25 Ultimate Experiences series, each conceived to whet your appetite for travel and for everything the world has to offer. As well as covering the globe, the 25s series also includes books on **Journeys, World Food, Adventure Travel, Places to Stay, Ethical Travel, Wildlife Adventures** and **Wonders of the World**.

When you start planning your trip, Rough Guides' new-look guides, maps and phrasebooks are the ultimate companions. For 25 years we've been refining what makes a good guidebook and we now include more colour photos and more information – on average 50% more pages – than any of our competitors. Just look for the sky-blue spines.

Rough Guides don't just travel – we also believe in getting the most out of life without a passport. Since the publication of the bestselling Rough Guides to **The Internet** and **World Music**, we've brought out a wide range of lively and authoritative guides on everything from **Climate Change** to **Hip-Hop**, from **MySpace** to **Film Noir** and from **The Brain** to **The Rolling Stones**.

Publishing information

Rough Guide 25 Ultimate experiences USA Published May 2007 by Rough Guides Ltd, 80 Strand, London WC2R 0RL
345 Hudson St, 4th Floor,
New York, NY 10014, USA
14 Local Shopping Centre, Panchsheel Park, New Delhi 110017, India
Distributed by the Penguin Group
Penguin Books Ltd,
80 Strand, London WC2R 0RL
Penguin Group (USA)
375 Hudson Street, NY 10014, USA
Penguin Group (Australia)
250 Camberwell Road, Camberwell,
Victoria 3124, Australia
Penguin Books Canada Ltd,
10 Alcorn Avenue, Toronto, Ontario,
Canada M4V 1E4
Penguin Group (NZ)
67 Apollo Drive, Mairangi Bay, Auckland
1310, New Zealand

Printed in China
© Rough Guides 2007
No part of this book may be reproduced in any form without permission from the publisher except for the quotation of brief passages in reviews.
80pp
A catalogue record for this book is available from the British Library
ISBN 978-1-84353-822-6
The publishers and authors have done their best to ensure the accuracy and currency of all the information in **Rough Guide 25 Ultimate experiences USA**, however, they can accept no responsibility for any loss, injury, or inconvenience sustained by any traveller as a result of information or advice contained in the guide.

1 3 5 7 9 8 6 4 2

Rough Guide credits

Editor: Amy Hegarty
Design & picture research: Michelle Bhatia
Cartography: Katie Lloyd-Jones, Maxine Repath

Cover design: Diana Jarvis, Chloë Roberts
Production: Aimee Hampson, Katherine Owers
Proofreader: Ella Steim

The authors

Ross Velton (Experiences 1, 18) contributes to Rough Guides to Florida and the USA; **Stephen Timblin** (Experiences 2, 4, 8) is author of the Rough Guide to Yellowstone and the Grand Tetons and a contributor to the Rough Guide to the USA; **JD Dickey** (Experiences 3, 9, 10, 11, 13, 15, Miscellany) is author of the Rough Guide to Los Angeles and co-author of Rough Guides to Seattle, California, Washington DC and the USA; **Zora O'Neill** (Experiences 5, 12, 14, 16), a New Mexico native, lives in New York City but travels extensively, in an attempt to taste every food in the world; **Caroline Lascom** (Experiences 6, 17) is a travel writer and editor based in Chicago; **Paul Whitfield** (Experiences 7, 25) is co-author of

the Rough Guide to Alaska and a contributor to the Rough Guide to the USA; **Stephen Keeling** (Experiences 19, 20, 21) has been exploring the backroads of the USA since 1991, after aiming for Mount Rushmore and ending up at the Crazy Horse Memorial instead; **Christian Williams** (Experiences 22) is author of the Rough Guide to Colorado and a contributor to the Rough Guide to the USA; **Sarah Hull** (Experiences 23) is a contributor to Rough Guides to Boston, New England and the USA; **Sean Harvey** (Experiences 24) is a freelance travel writer, jazz musician and voodoo enthusiast who revels publicly at every available opportunity.

Picture credits

Cover Neon cowgirl figure, Las Vegas, Nevada © Harald Sund/Getty Images

2 South Beach, Miami, FL at night © LOOK Die Bildagentur der Fotografen GmbH/Alamy

6 Grey wolf, Yellowstone National Park, WY © Jeff Vanuga/Corbis

8–9 South Beach, Miami, FL at night © LOOK Die Bildagentur der Fotografen GmbH/Alamy

10–11 Wrigley Field celebrations © Mark McMahon Photography, Franklin McMahon/Corbis

12–13 New York, NY © David Jay Zimmerman/Corbis

14 Grey wolf, Yellowstone National Park, WY © Jeff Vanuga/Corbis

16–17 Elvis Presley's Martin guitar; Elvis's green Cadillac convertible © Tod Gipstein/Corbis; Elvis's grave © Mark Perlstein/Time Life/Getty Images; Graffiti from fans on wall outside Graceland © Kevin Fleming/Corbis

18–19 30 May 1955, Indianapolis 500, IN © Bettmann/Corbis

20–21 Climbing Half Dome, Yosemite National Park © Micah May/Alamy

22 Skiing at Snowbird, UT© Karl Weatherly/Corbis

24–25 Civil Rights Memorial, Montgomery, AL © Philip Gould/Corbis; 14 Apr 1969, Dexter Avenue Baptist Church © Corbis

26–27 US Capitol at dusk © Visions of America, LCC/Alamy

28–29 Meridian vineyards, CA © Anita Delimont/Alamy; Newly harvested white grapes; Wine taster, Mondavi Winery, Napa Valley, CA © Charles O'Rear/Corbis

30–31 Open-pit wood barbecue near Austin, TX © Owen Franken/Corbis; Kielbasa sausage on barbecue grill © Owen Franken/Corbis; Meat barbecue © Owen Franken/Corbis

32–33 West of Logan Pass, Going-to-the-Sun Road, Glacier National Park, MT © Buddy Mays/Corbis

34–35 Christian church, Taos, NM © Adam Woolfitt/Corbis; Costumed Taos Indians attend a dance festival, NM © Adam Woolfitt/Corbis

36–37 Crabs on ice; Fresh shrimp © Martin Pernter; Seafood salesman at Pike Place Market, Seattle, WA © Kevin Schafer/Corbis; Fresh fish neon sign © Dave Bartruff/Corbis

38–39 Savannah's Victorian Gingerbread House © Stephanie Maze/Corbis

40–41 The First Baptist Church of South Londonderry, VT, in fall © Danita Delimont/Alamy

42–43 Roulette wheel © PSL Images/Alamy; Lucky sevens on a slot m achine © George B. Diebold/Corbis; Neon display in Glitter Gulch, Las Vegas, NV © Purcell Team/Alamy

44–45 The Mittens, Monument Valley, AZ © Phil Degginger/Alamy

46–47 Crazy Horse Memorial, Mount Rushmore, SD © Tim Thompson

48–49 Mount Pisgah, Blue Ridge Parkway, NC © David Muench/Corbis

50–51 Cross-country skiers, CO © Annie Griffiths Belt/Corbis

52–53 Portland Head Light at Fort Williams Park, Cape Elizabeth, ME © Chad Ehlers/Alamy; Eating lobster in Maine © Dean Conger/Corbis; Maine lobster dinner © Bob Krist/Corbis; Lobster Shack, Cape Elizabeth, ME © Robert Holmes/Corbis

54–55 Float at Mardi Gras, New Orleans, LA © Philip Gould/Corbis

57 Kayaking in Shoup Bay Marine State Park, Prince William Sound, AK © Alaska Stock LLC/Alamy

Fly Less – Stay Longer!

Rough Guides believes in the good that travel does, but we are deeply aware of the impact of fuel emissions on climate change. We recommend taking fewer trips and staying for longer. If you can avoid travelling by air, please use an alternative, especially for journeys of under 1000km/600miles. And always offset your travel at **www.roughguides.com/climatechange**.

Over 70 reference books and hundreds of travel
guides, maps & phrasebooks that cover the world